do
the
math

do
the
math

forms
emily galvin

T | P

Tupelo Press
Dorset, Vermont

COPYRIGHT

ACKNOWLEDGMENTS

To Robert Scanlan, Brighde Mullins, Zoe Savitsky, David Pincus, Noah Feehan, everyone who sacrificed eyesight and sanity to seek out the kinks and careless errors, and above all, Barry and Gretchen Mazur: thank you.

This book is for my grandmother.

CONTENTS

FORMS: CRYSTALLINE AND FLUID

Emily Galvin's poems, in *Do The Math*, are written in forms that have the grace of being intensely crystalline—in a way that I will describe in a moment—and yet these crystals, by their very nature, enact an organic unfolding.

Her poems are often in the guise of dramatic encounters, complete with stage directions. Many of them are dialogues recollecting missed opportunities, the loss made almost irrelevant by the clarity of the recollection itself. Some poems consist entirely of stage directions; the actors missing, yet the implied action all the more arresting; the stage manager patient:

> If there could be a little wind, that would be nice.

Love, of course, is what collects like evening dew on all these poems, and when it glistens in a full moon, is:

> like something seen once and never seen again—blue heron, sandhill crane

and is as surprising as the lover's "toenails full of sand."

These poems, as theater—as minute-long plays—often with a stage right and stage left, and lighting—force a majestic tempo to their reading. Galvin delights in the extraordinarily rich arithmetic of her novel poetic forms, making full use of the interplay between their crystalline and organic nature.

But all poetry banks on this interplay. The challenge, when you read the opening line of Thomas Gray's "Elegy Written in a Country Churchyard, "

> The Curfew tolls the knell of parting day,

is, on the one hand, to keep from tumbling into the deep groove of its intoning meter; and on the other, to respect, and not conceal, its music.

The line just quoted is in iambic pentameter, of course, the iamb consisting of a short syllable followed by a long syllable, ($\cup$ $-$), the various meanings of "short" and "long" to be discussed in a moment. But, whatever they mean, the template for the full line is

$\cup - \cup - \cup - \cup - \cup -$

When you label a line of poetry as iambic pentameter you are signaling, right there, a certain tension. The pentameter part of the description offers us up a clean number: five. That is, the line is thought to have 5 iambic feet. The iamb part of it, though, gives us a continuum of choices; for the combination "short-long" is a relative notion: whether the "short" part of the iamb measured against the "long" is in terms of duration, or stress, or a mixture, is unspecified in our description.

There is, in English or in any other language, no perfect iamb and even if there were, giving it five occurrences in the same line of poetry would stultify. A line like:

I summon up remembrance of things past

has no two of its five feet in quite the same iambic mold, and so is heard as in counterpoint with some ideal iambic pentameter *ta-dum ta-dum ta-dum ta-dum ta-dum*. This ideal can never, and of course should never, be realized.

We already have, then, in this staple metrical form iambic pentameter a marriage between the discrete (i.e., 5) and the continuous (i.e., the panoply of possible iambs). Discrete elements of poetical form I'll call *crystalline*, while continuous elements I'll call *fluid*. Line length in free verse is a somewhat fluid element of its form; the syllable count in Haiku is crystalline.

One of the evident differences between the crystalline and the fluid aspects of poetic form is in the manner of their evolution. We expect constant change, within the same poem, perhaps even within the same line, of the fluid; but any change in the crystalline signals either an evolution or a specific shattering of something within the particular poem, or else arises from some shift of grand tradition. The curtal-sonnets of Gerard Manley Hopkins, for example, with their $6 + 4 = 10$ lines and their half-line tails represents a cleanly marked departure from the proportion of octave and sextet in the $8 + 6 = 14$ line sonnets.

Is there some specific innate repertoire of crystalline forms within which poems can be written that have the power, if used well, to move us to tears, while other forms inevitably leave us cold? I think not; I think there is no limit; I think that any crystalline form suggests its (possibly slow, cultured) unfolding into something rich. Can you fashion, for example, a crystalline form out of a sequence of numbers as unprepossessing as:

7, 10, 6, 6, 8, 12, 6 ?

Marianne Moore built her poem "He Digesteth Harde Yron" out of it, or, at least, starting from its mold. Here is the first stanza:

> Although the aepyornis
> or roc that lived in Madagascar, and
> the moa are extinct,
> the camel-sparrow, linked
> with them in size—the large sparrow
> Xenophon saw walking by a stream—was and is
> a symbol of justice.

The sequence 7, 10, 6, 6, 8, 12, 6 are the number of syllables in each line, the two consecutive six-syllable lines being linked by an end-rhyme. This numerical pattern is repeated with variation, and minimal, but elegant, evolution in the nine stanzas of her poem so that it acquires emotional force, stanza by stanza. By the end of the poem—the last two lines of which are:

> This one remaining rebel
> is the sparrow-camel.

you think of the very crystalline form of her poem as standing for the skeletal architecture of this beast, sparrow or camel.

There are two major forms that Emily Galvin works with here; I'll refer to them by the names of two mathematicians, Fibonacci and Euclid.

Fibonacci (alias: Leonardo of Pisa) considered the interesting mathematical structure that arises if you were to have a community of creatures ("Fibonacci rabbits" they are fondly called) that procreated at a rate so that the number of individuals in each generation was the sum of the number of individuals of the two previous generations. So we have the sequence

$$1, 1, 2, 3, 5, 8, 13 \ldots$$

of successive census counts, where the initial 1, 1, represent the "Adam" and "Eve" of Fibonacci rabbithood. Galvin's poems in the Fibonacci form consist—most of the time—of a dialogue between, say, A and B, two characters sketched in an economy of pen strokes, about whom we know vividly perhaps only two things; namely,

• how well A knows B, and B knows A,
• how little A and B know each other,

and where, in their dialogue, each successive comment of A, or of B, is a distillation or a combination, or a refutation, or a glancing comment on, no more than the two previous lines of their interchange. The form, then, is elegantly focusing on how a shared understanding builds between them, and yet how it never does. Almost in emotional contradiction to all this, however, a Fibonacci-like energy pulses in the (pro-)creation of their dialogue. This is trenchantly enacted in the very form (the "math") of their speech, either in the pattern 1, 1, 2, 3, 5, 8, 13... of the number of words in a line, or the number of words in the sentences (taking into account that they sometimes finish each other's sentence) or in the stanza structure of their conversation.

Euclid began and ended Book VII of his Elements of Geometry by discussing a process—now known as the Euclidean Algorithm—where, starting with two numbers A and B, via successive operations of subtraction, you can arrive at a determination of the largest number C that is a divisor of A and of B (a greatest common divisor of A and B)[1].

In Emily Galvin's Euclidean Algorithm poems, the interlocutors A and B refine their utterances, successive subtractions being the mode of propulsion of their dialogue, and "the math" drives them on to a common distillation.

A cornucopia of still other mathematical elements glisten through the poetry. One poem is entwined in a spiral; the stately, yet ornery, sequence of prime numbers 2, 3, 5, 7, 11, 13, ... quietly counts the spaces between words in the lines of another. And as is true of mathematics, all of Galvin's work—fluid and crystalline—is in the service of passion.

—BARRY MAZUR
Gerhard Gade University Professor
Mathematics Department, Harvard University

---

[1]For example, the greatest common divisor of 18 and 12 is 6; in this simple instance the Euclidean Algorithm boils down to telling you simply to subtract 12 from 18 to get the answer. But if you applied the Euclidean algorithm to get the greatest common divisor of, say, 4001 and 691, the Euclidean algorithm would have you perform a hefty number of subtractions to get the answer, which happens, actually, to be 1.

SPIRAL

```
I F E E L L I K E T H E S   G L O V E B O X
M A R T E S T K I D O N T   . S U R E , Y O
H E S H O R T B U S . I M   U R E L E C T R
P O S S I B L E R E L A T   O N I C L A D Y
I O N S H I P S . T H E W   J U M P S T H E
H E E L I S S P I N N I N   G U N F R O M T
G B U T T H E H A M S T E   I M E T O T I M
R L O N G S I N C E D I E   E , & S T I L L
D . T H I S T I M E T H E   I S T   I N S T R
Y D E C I D E D T O M A K   A N I   U M E N T
E T H E D E A F K I D P L   I N S   — I N T E
A Y M U S I C A L C H A I   I D I   L L E C T
R S . N I G H T F A L L S   O U S   I N T H E
I N T H E D I T C H . I S T H I S E X I S
T E N T I A L O R D E V O U T ? T H E R E
W A S A T I M E W H E N I T H O U G H T P
A N I C W A S D I V I N E . T R O U B L E
I S , I C A N ' T R E C O G N I Z E F I G
M E N T S O F Y O U R I M A G I N A T I O
N . A B J E C T S U B J E C T I V I T Y ,
A S T H E M A N M I G H T S A Y . L O N G
F E L L O W S A I D , " T H E L E A V E S
O F M E M O R Y S E E M E D T O M A K E A
M O U R N F U L R U S T L I N G I N T H E
D A R K . " L E A V E S , A S H E S , A R
O S E B Y A N Y O T H E R N A M E — T H E
P O I N T I S , H E C A N ' T R E M E M B
E R W H E R E H E S P E N T T H E N I G H
T . T H I S I S W H A T H A P P E N S W H
E N Y O U ' R E M A K I N G O T H E R P L
A N S . T H E S E A R E T H E A S P I R A
T I O N S O F T H E H O L Y G H O S T . A
N Y O N E C A N F I N D O U T W H E N W E
W E R E E A T E N B Y T H E S A I N T S .
```

PREMISE

A stage. Hardwood floor long since warped, forcing ridges in the thick polyurethane finish and, in some places, leaving gaps. The lights highlight the nicks in the finish.

Curtain, legs, drop: all black velvet, all gray with dust.

The stage curves out into the house, three steps descending on either side. If there were footlights, they would mark roughly one-eighth of a circle fifty feet in diameter, and stand somewhere in the neighborhood of three-and-a-half feet high. In the house, the floor is made of vinyl—the same bloodless not-quite-linoleum-but-close style of off-white squares that define the interior aesthetic of American public schools.

At the moment, there is no audience but the chairs. Bolted-down chairs with folding seats, rounded tops and metal backs, upholstered in coarse red cloth. A deep shade of burgundy meant for the elegance of operas, a rough breed of fabric intended for grain sacks and military Spam. Something in the burlap family. In one or two seats, growing tears reveal an interior of yellow foam.

Two aisles divide these chairs into three sections, the sides one-half the breadth of the section between the aisles. The vinyl ascends at an angle of roughly 10° to meet two sets of heavy double doors, each set operable only by a push-bar mechanism, which is somewhat awkward to open and incomprehensibly loud to close. Between the doors, planted at the back of the middle seats, there is a small booth, from which the lights are operated. Most of it's taken up by an enormous spotlight, which may never have been used. Beside the heavy canister of the spot, there is a tall metal stool, which sits before a light-operator's control board, its switches marked with colored tape. Clutter surrounds the neatly delineated board on all available sides—(gels, paper, posters, spike tape, scissors, old clothes, candy wrappers, boxes, admonitions, pens, markers, piles of scrap cloth, etc.).

On either side of the stage stand two aspen trees. The bark is white or graying, thin, puckered with raised black circles. The dust of the aspen trees would be about the same shade as the dust that covers the black drop and legs. They are middle-aged aspens—their trunks not thicker in diameter than 8 inches. They are growing out of the stage, raising and cracking the shellac and wood around their roots. They are, actually, the same tree—like most aspen groves, their roots meet and join underground, so that what appear to be many trees are actually one. It is fall for these trees, and their leaves are flaming red and gold. Their leaves appear to be lit from within. In the room, the light is slanting and yellow. This is winter afternoon light, the light that hits an Iowa cornfield at about 3:00 pm on a sunny day in February. Very deep slant, very warm yellow. It is hitting the aspens in pieces.

If there could be a little wind, that would be nice.

FIBONACCI VIGNETTE

Two men. A porch. Coming winter.

A small town in the Midwest. Iowa or Illinois, maybe eastern Nebraska. The two men are dressed for the cold in coats whose ability to provide warmth expired about fifteen years back. It could be any time after 1950. They are sitting on a porch, in creaky outside chairs. Maybe plastic, maybe wood. They are sitting on the porch of an old farmhouse, which is painted a color somewhere between half-dry cement and a winter river (known on paint chips as Turtledove Gray.) The sky is also gray, but a much whiter shade—it does not appear clouded, but blank.

Black. Whirring sound of an old projector. The words IT BEGINS AT ZERO appear, then disappear, followed by the words ADD ONE.

> FIRST
>
> Mm.

> SECOND
>
> Oh?

> FIRST
>
> Seen her?

> SECOND
>
> Seen her today.

> FIRST
>
> What was she wearing, today?

> SECOND
>
> A dress—blue, darker—no stockings, no
> coat. She looked nice, I tell you what...she
> always looked nicest in blue.

> FIRST
>
> The last time I saw her she was wearing a
> blue coat, with a little hat on—

> SECOND
>
> Last time it snowed.

FIRST

So I went out this morning, early this
morning, still dark, and went down to the
Agency, and got in line—

SECOND

Still nothing—

FIRST

Still nothing, nothing and nothing I can do
about it anyway. I could have been the first,
but hell—her hair—

SECOND

It was loose, around her shoulders—

FIRST

—It was nice loose—

SECOND

But she came by quick and didn't stop to say
hello, just a quick smile and that was it—I
was in line—

FIRST

—And she wasn't stopping there, not like
that—

SECOND

—No, not like that.

A moment.
The sound of the projector again, and the words IT GOES appear, then disappear.
The image tears away, like the end of an 8mm tape reel—the house, the porch, the men are
gone. Just whirring white. Then, in black type:

Fibonacci Sequence: The infinite sequence
of numbers beginning 1, 1, 2, 3, 5, 8, 13,… in
which each term is the sum of the two terms
preceding it. The ratio of successive

Fibonacci terms tends to the golden ratio, namely, $\dfrac{1+\sqrt{5}}{2}$

The words disappear and everything goes black.

END

EUCLID'S ALGORITHM

These ten scenes happen on the blank stage.
A and B could be any two people, so long as
they've been together for longer than either
can remember.

O N E

A.

I love you.

B.

I know.

Pause

A.

What was that?
You know? *(Leaving)* Oh.

B.

I know.
So? Oh.

T W O

A.

What am I going to do now?

B.

Don't know—the same?

Pause

A.

I don't know what to do now.
I can't keep going. (*Leaving*) Still, probably will.

B.

Are you all right?
What's the matter? *(Leaving)* Everyone—

A.

It's not them.
I just can't.

THREE

A.

When was it that we were last here?

B.

It was summer.

Pause

A.

Was that the last time we were here?
That first summertime? It can't be. *(Leaving)*
That long?

B.
I think so.
Time flies. *(Leaving)* Evaporates.

A.

That long.
Nothing's changed.

FOUR

A.

I'm exhausted—let's just call it a night,
alright?

B.

I don't really think I'm ready to go to bed yet
at all.

Pause

B.

But don't wait up just because I'm not ready
to go to bed.
If you're exhausted, you just call it a night.
(*Leaving*) I'm going to read.

A.

I think I will, actually, I'll go to bed.
You're going to read? Just…going to read.
(*Leaving*) Goodnight.

B.

Just go to bed.
Have a good night.

FIVE

*Lights up on A. and B. They sit in two gray
folding chairs, facing out, feet straight ahead,
hands on knees, looking at the floor.*

*A. looks at B. A. moves foot towards B. A.
closes knees. A. looks away.*

*B. looks at A. B. looks where A. is looking.
B. looks down.*

Pause

*A. looks at B. A. moves foot towards B. A.
closes knees. A. looks away.*
*B. looks at A. B. looks where A. is looking.
(Leaving) B. puts one foot behind the other.*

*B. looks at A. B. looks where A. is looking.
B. looks down.*
A. looks at B. A. looks at B.'s feet.
They try to kiss, but cannot reach.

S I X

Lights up on N. entering stage left. N. stops, freezes, starts walking again.

N.

When I first saw you it was night, on the beach, with a full moon overhead, and the light from the moon bounced off the water into your hair so that all I could see was the light of the top of your head, making a silver outline down by the water, moving in the wind. *(N. stops, turns, looks back, continues)*

I was walking through fields of rough grass, this tough, sharp grass that tore at my legs, and I couldn't find my way through to the beach—I had gone off the path in the dark—and I crossed dune after dune through these splinters of grass, and I thought I would never get there *(glances out)* but I had gone too far from the path to find my way back now, and just then I came over a big dune and there you were, on the wide, white sand, with the wind and the light all in your hair.

Pause

(Walking harder now) I was walking through that sharp, stiff grass and it was cutting little tiny slivers in my skin, and I had been walking for miles or maybe just in circles, miles of circles, but when I crossed over that last big dune and saw you down by the water, with the wind and the light in your hair, I thought that maybe all that distance had not been over land at all, but somehow I had wandered in to elsewhere, somehow through the saw grass I had crossed through the clouds and there you were, walking, all alone.

(Stops. Turns. Delivers back:) When I first saw you that night, on the beach, with a full moon overhead, you were wearing a pale dress, a light fabric of a pale color that blew in the wind, it blew back between your legs and out behind you as you walked, and the bottom was heavy with salt water and sand. *(Leaving)* The way I loved you then, like something seen once and never seen again—blue heron, sandhill crane—I never imagined walking down to see your toenails full of sand—I had no mind to imagine loving you from anything but far. *(Turns back. Keeps walking.)*

From the top of that big dune in the cutting-grass, I stood looking at you with the wind and the light in your hair, and still never thought of pushing down and closer—never imagined loving you from anything but far, and still, even close enough to see the waves within your hair, still—I—remain.

It got colder, sand like a marble pool, the sun gone down now—I remember wondering if the horizon would flash green, still I never looked away, not even then—like standing at the end of the world to look for something new. *(Leaving)* The grass left cuts, splayed weblike, and I felt the blood begin to bead.

There's an end I don't remember anymore. I must, at some point, have lost sight, and come home and lit a fire, and then—and I may not have thought of it then, but if I did—even then, I didn't know.

What was it that drew me through the grass and down those sandy banks? What was it that drew me from the road and through those saw-edged fields? What was it that drew me from bed and pulled me to the sea?
(N. exits stage right. Lights down.)

SEVEN

*Lights up on A. and B. facing each other, A.
looking down. A moment.*

*B. looks at the ceiling. B. looks back at A.
B. moves hand towards A. B. moves slightly
towards A.*

*A. looks at B. B. freezes. B. brings feet
together.*

Pause

*B. looks at the ceiling. B. looks back at A.
B. moves hand towards A. B. moves slightly
towards A.*

*A. looks at B. B. freezes. B. brings feet
together. (Leaving) A. opens mouth.*

*A small sound escapes A. B. looks down.
A. closes mouth.*

*A. cracks a knuckle with the thumb of the
same hand. B. winces. A. looks away.*

EIGHT

A.

Well, are you coming with me?

B.

I don't know what I'm going to do.

Pause

A.

What do you think you're going to do?
Do you think you'll come over? *(Leaving)*
Later on?

B.

I dunno if I'll come now.
Later on? Later when? We'll see.

NINE

A.

When I went out this morning, there was the
most beautiful sky—even though it was dark
and gray, it was so beautiful… it smelled
so good.

B.

I'm sorry I missed it.

Pause

A.

I saw it through the window when I woke up,
and I thought it would rain—but I went out
anyway, and it—I wish you'd come.
Where were you this morning? Did you go
out today? It doesn't matter, never mind. I'm
sorry you missed it. It was really something
else. *(Leaving)* Missed you.

B.

I haven't even been out.
I should. Next time. *(Leaving)* Soon.

A.

Sure. Wait!
Listen—rain.

TEN

B.

So I looked for you, looked all over, called
your name, looked outside—I couldn't find
you anywhere. Where were you?

A.

I was here, same as always.

Pause

B.

Are you sure?—I could have sworn I looked
everywhere—how could you not have
heard me? I called and called.
So you were here, like always? Do you have
trouble hearing here? Maybe I was outside
the house. *(Leaving)* I don't know.

A.

I go to the pier sometimes.
Hear the birds. Then come home.

Onto the black back wall, the following slides are projected, words in white.

(Slide 1:)

Algorithm: A process, or set of rules, usually one expressed in algebraic notation.

(Slide 2:)

Euclid's Algorithm: An algorithm for finding the greatest common divisor (GCD) of two numbers. It relies on the identity

$$\gcd(a, b) = \gcd(a-b, b)$$

(Slide 3:)

To find the GCD of two numbers by this algorithm, repeatedly replace the larger by subtracting the smaller from it until the two numbers are equal.

The slide flickers to black.

END

EUCLID'S ALGORHYTHM

SHORT STORY: *The camera pans around the inside of a log cabin, somewhere around nowhere's northern projects.*

LONG STORY: *The camera pans across the inside of a log cabin. This cabin doesn't come in a kit. It was built by hand, and built well. The logs are round, long and straight, with dovetailed corners. The chinking is smooth and carefully done. The ceiling is supported by two crossbeams, eight-inch thick boards that stretch from wall to wall, edge down, with three of the same cut so that each crossbeam appears to have a star bursting on its back. Above these crossbeams, the roof is loud metal. If there were even a drop of rain, it would echo throughout the house. The house is quiet.*

This room is the kitchen. Medium shot of the southern portion, shot from the very center of the room. The floor is linoleum. The kitchen table is dark wood covered in a checkered cloth. Below the cloth, the legs are an intricate network of shapes and carving, marred by a few visible axe marks, where the table was attacked. Most of the axe marks are covered by the tablecloth. The chairs around the table are in pairs—no more than two of them match. They are old, and only one of them is comfortable. The comfortable chair, a wood-frame padded-seat chair covered in a blue saddle blanket, stands at the western head of the table, next to the wood and white metal cabinet, visible in the corner of the frame. This cabinet is actually a sort of dresser with a cabinet sitting on top of it. It contains everything. The table stands at the side of the room, between the southeast and southwest corners. Along the southern wall are two large windows.

The camera begins to pan right. In the southeast corner, the south wall is covered in beat-up coats. The eastern wall is covered in a large, light-pink patchwork quilt, a flying geese pattern. It has a few tears, where the white inside shows through. Along the top of this quilt hang various hats and bits—caps, bonnets, sunhats, a snaffle bit, a reining snaffle, and a curb, hanging on the same hook as a leather hackamore.

The camera is now facing the eastern side of the room, finishing a slow 90° turn. The front door, wood with three narrow, horizontal windows of descending length, stands slightly south of the middle of the eastern wall.

Cut to medium shot, from same center position, of opposite wall, the western wall. Across from it, there is another door, leading down a short stair to other rooms. This door, unlike the front door, wasn't there when the cabin was originally built. It was cut out later, and therefore has no frame, but shows the big circles of log-ends on either side.

North, a wooden counter with a marble top juts out from the western wall about four feet east. Above the counter's end, on the wall, is a stained glass window showing a sunrise. The camera pans right now, and follows the counter, which continues along the western wall, containing a sink, above which there are piles of papers on nails and feathers stuck in all the cracks of the logs. Every feather is sacred in its own way. The papers are letters from friends, and one typed copy of a poem. Above these letters is a black frame containing an unknown soldier's memorial made of handkerchiefs sent from France, and surrounding this are various old pictures and postcards.

The counter then bends around the northern wall, which, above the counter, is covered in pans. The camera continues the turn. There is a third door in the center of this wall. It, too, was cut out, and shows the logs on either side. One side of the door contains the height chart of a child, now grown. On the other side of the door hang more papers, more pans, and a medium-sized print of "When Do You Marry?" by Gauguin. More postcards, a third-place ribbon. Things on this side of the wall are a bit blackened, because this corner is dominated by a large, old, wood-burning stove. The stove is this: a large box, green and white, which contains the fire, the ashes, and an oven. It stands on four green legs, sage green, light. The top of this box is a black stovetop, thick and containing a multiplicity of ways to disassemble. There is then a green frame, supporting a shelf above the stove which is covered in spice-bottles and a small pile of pot-holders. Behind the shelf, an eight-inch thick black stovepipe rises through the roof. On the other side of the stove, on the eastern wall by the front door, are a wood-box, a few brooms, various rags on nails.

The camera has now returned to the front door. Tilting up, the camera reveals the space above the door. Above the front door are some small dolls, hanging on the wall. Jump cut to a shot of the space above the western door. Above the western door is a wooden diamondback rattler—made by a child from a single, narrow board—and long, narrow frames of very old photographs.

Cut to black. In green letters, the words:
> The room is warm and there are trees outside.

Dissolve to black.

Cut to shot of kitchen table. GREATER and LESSER are sitting at the table. LESSER is sitting in the comfortable chair.

GREATER

There's nothing nice about this winter wind.

LESSER

You didn't have to stay.

Pause

GREATER

There isn't anywhere I'd rather be.
There wasn't any choice. *(Leaving)* I had to stay.

LESSER

You haven't been much use.
Not bad, today. *(Leaving)* The wind.

GREATER

It hasn't grown.
Same. And cold.

Cut to black.

10 seconds go by.

Fade in to the same shot. This time GREATER is in the comfortable chair.

GREATER

I never saw a sky that white till now. It's
gone from gray to paler gray to pale. And all
the while the colder.

LESSER

It's always white like this, this time of year.

Pause

GREATER

There wasn't wind like this, the years before.
It blew, and it blew cold, but not this hard.
And it's just coming on.
A long, hard snow would do the grass some
good. Without some water, the summer's
going to burn. *(Leaving)* The spring is going
down.

LESSER

If it goes dry, we'll haul it up from town.
How much has it gone down? *(Leaving)* Could it
go dry?

GREATER

It hasn't in my life.
But who's to say. *(Leaving)* It could.

LESSER

And if it does?
The water? We'll burn.

GREATER and LESSER regard each other. Fade to shot of aspen trees outside. 10 seconds.
Cut to black.

END

RHINESTONE HAIR CLIP
Trisection of the Angle

Lights up. Dark hardwood floors are covered by cheap oriental rugs. At the center of the stage, facing the back wall, a couch. The couch is a dull brownish greenish grayish shade, covered in pillows, some of them also oriental. It's a little broken down. The kind of couch that, when you sit in it, it's hard to get out of. Lights down.

Lights up on ANN, frantically searching for something in the couch. Tossing pillows aside, she tears the room apart. She tries to put the room back together as she goes, but only succeeds in a forced-looking semblance of its prior state.

ANN
Fuck. Fuck fuck fuck fuck—where the fuck? God—*dammit.* It was fucking right there. Motherfucking cocksucker. Where the fuck, what, it fucking got up and *left?!?...* SHIT.

She stops and covers her face with both hands, in frustration

Enter BEN. He picks a spot, maybe four feet into the room, and stands there without moving.

BEN
(Through a peanut butter and jelly sandwich he is eating) Whatcha lookin' for?

ANN
(Distracted, as she has resumed her search) My fucking... um... hang on... my... thingy... y'know... that... um... *(Momentarily pauses from searching)* Sorry. That hairclip Cactus gave me for Christmas. I got it like two days ago and it's already fucking gone. *(Resumes her search)* I feel really lousy about it anyway. I really liked that crappy little thing.

BEN
Where'd'ya last see it?

ANN
I don't know. On my head. Or on the table. I don't know... *(Stops again)* see, I take it out, when I play with my hair, and I could have taken it out anywhere. *(Resumes searching, going through drawers now)* I think I had it at dinner. Did I have it at dinner?

BEN

(Chewing) Whassit look like?

ANN

It's um, it's purple and kind of sparkly… like it's diamonds but… it's not… they're fake and plasticky. It's shaped like a bug… a… um… y'know, the long bugs?

BEN

Long bugs?

ANN

(Stops) Yeah, long…like butterflies but long and skinny.

BEN

Dragonflies?

ANN

(Resumes) I don't know. Maybe. Anyway I really liked it and it was really pretty and it was purple, which looks really nice in my hair, and I can't *fucking* find it anywhere.

BEN

Where have you looked?

ANN

Where do you think I've looked? Fucking everywhere. The couch, the floor, under the furniture… why? Did you see it somewhere?

BEN

No. I didn't see it. *(Sandwich finished)* Hey, do you have my Rush CD?

ANN

What?

BEN

My Rush CD. Can't find it.

ANN

No. Why would I want your fucking crappy Rush CD?

BEN

That's what I was thinking.

ANN

(Absentmindedly, while going through more drawers) Did you check the CD player upstairs?

BEN

No.

ANN

Did you check the car?

BEN

No.

ANN

Cactus's CD book? He has sticky fingers, even with shit he doesn't want.

BEN

No.

ANN

(Stopping and turning to him) Well where the fuck have you looked, then?

Pause

BEN

Um, not anywhere, really. I guess I just sort of thought it would turn up.

Pause

ANN

You're an idiot. (Resumes searching)

BEN takes a Kodak instant camera from his back pocket, snaps a picture of ANN rummaging. She doesn't notice. He takes another picture, checks how many pictures he has left. He takes a picture of his feet. Stops, shaking the camera slightly like a Polaroid picture. He looks around the room. Snaps a photo of the ceiling fan. Starts framing a picture of his left hand, to be taken with his right. Ann finishes the last drawer and turns to go back to the couch, towards BEN. She stops.

ANN

What the fuck are you doing?

BEN

Taking pictures.

ANN

Of *what*?

BEN

Myself. The room. (*Pause*) You.

ANN

Me? You took a picture of me? When?

BEN

A minute ago.

ANN

What was I doing?

BEN

I dunno. You were over there at the cabinet going through drawers and shit.

ANN

Well that's stupid. You took a picture of my back crouched over a drawer.

BEN

You looked nice. It was meaningful.

ANN

Fuck you.

BEN

Find that hair clip?

ANN

NO! What the fuck, Ben, no! You asshole. I fucking hate you right now.

BEN

What?

41

ANN

You are just so fucking unhelpful and you don't care about shit and I don't know.
You are just generally being an asshole and on top of that you're being weird about
it. I mean, Jesus Christ, who takes a picture of… I don't fucking know what. You're
just fucking beyond me. What the fuck are you trying to do?

BEN

I'm not trying to do anything. I'm trying to help you find your thingy.

ANN

No, Ben, you're fucking not. You're not helping. You're taking pictures with your
stupid little throw-away camera, and you're not helping anybody.

BEN

Jeez. I'm sorry. (*Pause*) Where do you want me to look? (*Goes towards the other side
of the room, starts looking at an armchair. He bends over and gets really close to it but doesn't
touch it or move the cushions around, not because he's facetious about helping but just because
he honestly has no idea how to look for things.*) I don't see it.

ANN

(*Coming over to him*) Of course you don't fucking see it. It's small. It would fall
between the cushions… fuck it. It's not here. It's just a stupid little fake plastic
barrette, okay? Let's not worry about it. I'm sorry I bitched you out—I'm just a little
stressed out right now.

BEN

No, no, it's okay, um, we'll find it, okay? Just, um, why don't you go upstairs and
chill? I don't know, watch some TV or something. I'll look down here and in the
kitchen. (*She hesitates*) I have to look for my Rush CD anyway, remember?

ANN

(*Exhausted, down*) Okay. (*Pause, long pause*) Thanks, Ben.

BEN

No problem. Git.

He slaps her on the butt as she heads toward the door.

*BEN waits, staring at where she went. We hear ANN going up stairs and then we hear
footsteps above. BEN waits until there are creaks overhead. He turns, looks at the armchair.
He sits. He stares out in front of him. Then, without moving his eyes from the point in space*

on which they've been fixed, slowly brings his left hand to his right breast pocket. He pulls out a small, purple, rhinestone hair clip, shaped like a dragonfly. He brings his hand, dragonfly in it, to his lap. He lays his left hand on his open right hand. He looks down at his hands, at the hair clip. Twenty seconds goes by in this position.

BEN

(Without moving anything but his mouth, calling to upstairs) I can't find it!

Lights down.

END

WENDOVER

Describe All Solutions To The Problem $x^2 + y^2 = z^2$

Wendover is a border town. The western half of town is in Nevada, the eastern half in Utah. Needless to say, the line down the middle is bright and distinct. The western side of town flourishes, full of casinos, restaurants, shops, and chains, full of people. The eastern half is a run-down-and-out string of cheap hotels with bad carpeting and leaky roofs, an effort at sinlessness falling far short of pristine.

Lights up. A hotel room. The bed is center stage, foot pointing toward the audience. Stage left of the bed there is a little desk with a mirror hanging above it, and a chair. Upstage right of the bed, we see the beginnings of a hotel bathroom, a counter with two sinks and another, bigger mirror. Near this counter sits a crumpled duffle bag.

HELEN stands in front of the mirror that hangs on the wall behind the little hotel desk, stage left, carefully applying makeup. Behind her, WILLIS sits on the downstage edge of the bed. He stares straight ahead, hands clasped in his lap. He may or may not have a slight, asymmetrical facial tic.

She draws her materials from a pile she has on the desk. She starts with a clean face, which she picks at briefly before laying down some industrial-strength foundation. She applies it with a sponge, a triangular sponge that comes off a stack she has, wrapped in plastic. Over the foundation, she begins dabbing spots of concealer. The concealer is very thick and requires some sculpting. Next, she gets to work on her eyes, which she pulls into grotesque shapes in order to curl her lashes and apply eyeliner, shadow in her creases, pale highlights on her brow bone and lower lid. She then piles on copious amounts of mascara, turning the brush perpendicular to her face to clump it on with the tip of the mascara wand. Last, she applies a stick of day-glo pink lipstick, directly from the tube. She puts on coat after coat, which is difficult while speaking.

HELEN

Are you ready?

WILLIS

Yes.

HELEN

Do you have your shoes on?

WILLIS gets up, and goes back towards the bathroom to get his shoes.

HELEN

I swear to God, it takes you longer to get ready to go than anyone I've ever known.

WILLIS returns to the end of the bed, sits down, begins unlacing a shoe.

HELEN

Are you driving?

WILLIS

I can drive.

WILLIS puts his left shoe on, tightens, and ties it.

HELEN

Where do you want to go?

WILLIS

(Unlacing his right shoe) I thought we'd just drive around until we found somewhere.

HELEN

I want a steak.

WILLIS puts his right shoe on, tightens, ties.

HELEN

A really good one. Juicy. Bloody. With mashed potatoes and rolls. And cake. Definitely cake.

WILLIS

Well, we can do that.

HELEN

Do you know anywhere we can get that?

WILLIS

No.

HELEN

Does the hotel have a restaurant?

WILLIS

I don't think so. It's an Express.

HELEN

Oh.

She begins putting on earrings. They are extremely difficult to attach.

HELEN

What about the Rainbow? The place we saw coming in? They looked nice.

WILLIS

We can go anywhere you want.

Something occurs to WILLIS. He gets up, goes to his bag which is by the bathroom. He pulls out a ragged child's doll and carries it to the edge of the bed. He sits, holding it. HELEN does not notice.

HELEN

What do you want to do after?

WILLIS

I don't know.

HELEN

I wonder if there's dancing. I'd like to go dancing.

WILLIS

I bet there's dancing somewhere.

HELEN

Do you think so? I'd really like that. Or maybe we could go to a movie. Did you see a theater coming into town?

WILLIS

I didn't see one, but I can check at the desk.

WILLIS looks at the doll. He looks to his right. He looks back at the doll as he stands. He considers it. He walks over to the stage right side of the bed, and slips it just under the bed— within reach, but hidden. He returns to the end of the bed, resumes sitting.

HELEN

What time do you want to leave in the morning?

WILLIS

I thought I'd let you sleep in.

HELEN

Could we have breakfast?

WILLIS

I don't know. Maybe. Maybe I'll just go out and get something.

HELEN

Oh, breakfast in bed would be great!

WILLIS

There's a coffeemaker in the room.

HELEN

Is there? That stuff's terrible anyway. Maybe we should go out.

WILLIS

Whatever you feel like in the morning.

WILLIS glances slightly to his right, as if a fly just hit his ear. HELEN turns from her mirror.

HELEN

I love you.

WILLIS

I love you, too.
Lights down.

ENDING 1:

Lights up on the empty hotel room. Enter WILLIS. He comes in hurriedly and goes straight to the side of the bed. He kneels. He looks under the bed where he put the doll. He picks up the doll. He turns. He looks at the door. He looks at the doll. He puts the doll back under the bed and hurries back out the door, shutting it carefully behind him. Lights down.

ENDING 2:

Lights up on the empty hotel room. Enter WILLIS. He comes in hurriedly and goes straight to the side of the bed. He kneels. He looks under the bed where he put the doll. He reaches for it but it isn't there. Frantically, he goes to the other side of the bed, feeling for the doll. Still nothing. He goes to his bag, rummages. Nothing. He looks at the door, looks at his bag, looks at the bed. He freezes. Lights down.

ENDING 3:

Lights don't go down. HELEN turns, looks at WILLIS.

HELEN

Are you ready?

WILLIS

I'm ready. Let's go.

They leave, HELEN going out first. Before he shuts the door, WILLIS pauses, looking back towards the side of the bed. Lights down.

ENDING 4:

Pick up at the end of ENDING 3. The door re-opens. WILLIS re-enters.

WILLIS

(Over his shoulder) I'll be right there!

He goes into the room, in the dark. Feels under the bed. Pulls his hand out from under the bed and crouches, silent and still. A small noise escapes his throat. Blackout.

ENDING 5:

Lights up on WILLIS, alone in the room. He is standing in the center of the room, holding the doll limply in his outstretched left hand. He is staring wildly out at the audience. Blackout.

ENDING 6:

Lights up on the empty hotel room. Enter HELEN. She leaves the door open behind her. She goes to WILLIS'S bag, looks in, rummages, finds nothing. She goes to the chest of drawers and looks through them. She stops. She puts her hands on her hips. She looks around at the floor. She catches sight of the bed. She goes to the bed at the foot and looks under. She sees the doll up by the side of the bed. She crawls on her hands and knees over to the doll. She takes the doll out. She presses the doll to her chest. She looks furtively around her. Slowly, she stands and goes to the door. She stops, looking out the open door. Blackout.

ENDING 7:

Lights up on HELEN and WILLIS. They are sitting on opposite sides of the bed, backs to one another, feet on the floor. The doll is in HELEN'S lap. A moment. HELEN looks over her shoulder at WILLIS. WILLIS looks at the floor. Blackout.

END

THEY CAME HOME

Doubling of the Cube

Lights up.

LILY is sitting stage left, with her head on her arms, which are folded on the kitchen table in front of her, not moving. Her left arm is over her right arm. The heat is making a hissing noise somewhere behind the counters. After a minute, she slowly looks up. She looks directly ahead, which is towards stage right. She lifts her head only slightly, so much that her lips press against her left wrist. In doing this, she lifts only her head, without un-hunching her back. Her eyebrows are slightly raised, wrinkling her forehead as she stares ahead. She lowers her eyes to stare at the table directly in front of her left arm. She breathes deeply in through her nose, and out through her nose, the breath amplified against her arm. She brings her head down again so that her head rests on her right eye-socket, into which her left wrist is pressing. In this position, she scrunches up her face into an extreme grimace. She holds this for twenty seconds. She relaxes her face, and in doing so a small noise escapes the back of her throat. She pushes her face back between her arms. She remains.

Enter DONALD. He enters stage right, across the table from where LILY is sitting. He stops. He looks at her.

DONALD

Hey.

No response.

DONALD

Are you okay?

No response.

DONALD

Um, okay.

DONALD begins going about the kitchen to make himself a sandwich, getting peanut butter and jelly out of the fridge, a plate from a cabinet, and a knife from a drawer. He is very careful with the spreading.

DONALD

D'you want a sandwich? I just got this new peanut butter—creamy—do you like creamy? I think I remember you liking creamy. I don't like the nuts. I mean, I think I'd like them better if I was doing something else with the peanut butter, but in a PB and J, I don't know. It kind of clashes. With the jelly? It's like, too much for the jelly. Anyway, Andrew kept buying that hippie crap. Not only was it crunchy, it did this weird thing where if you left it sitting in the cabinet too long, this layer of oil would accumulate on the top. And then you had to stir it before you could use it again. I mean, what the fuck? That's like, you might as well just make your own fucking peanut butter at that point. You're crushing fucking nuts and mixing it yourself. You pretty much just bought a jar.

LILY simultaneously raises her head and her hands, so that her head rises to meet her palms, which she places in her eye sockets. She then rubs her hands down her face, so that her palms reach her chin, slightly tilting her head back to facilitate the process. In the same motion, she rubs her hands back up her face, in a V so that her palms wind up on her temples, fingers meeting above her forehead. Elbows on table, still slouching, the pressure between her hands holding up her head.

DONALD

(Bringing his sandwich to the table, he sits in the up right chair, facing the audience.) That's not as bad as the shit he used to buy, though. Before he went on this hippie kick, he used to buy that peanut-butter-and-jelly-in-one shit? With the swirls? That was bad. The peanut butter wasn't bad, actually, it was okay. I think the stuff was made by a peanut butter company. But the jelly—Jesus. That shit was lethal. Horrible. It was like, if you could just unroll the peanut-butter-and-jelly swirl, you could probably have lifted the jelly off in one sheet. It was like cafeteria icing. Terrible. Way too sweet, with a rubbery thing going on—man. That was bad. At least now he's concerned about the potential toxicity of his food. And he makes some pretty decent shit now and again. I mean, vegan food is generally awful, that's just a given. But some of the stuff he makes is less awful than you'd expect.

LILY brings her elbows in towards her body, sliding them across the table. In doing this, her palms travel down her face again, tugging her skin into a saggy mask. Back straightening and eyes toward the sky, she rubs her fingertips under her eyes, her hands now together over her nose and mouth. She releases a deep breath, amplified by her hands. It sounds like this is the first one she's let out in a while. She allows her fingers to clasp, her wrists bending so that, elbows together on the table, back straight, clasped hands at the base of her face, she comes close to looking prim. Her lips rest on her hands, slightly smushing. She looks at DONALD.

DONALD

(Mouth full) You sure you don't want anything?

LILY nods.

DONALD

I need milk. *(He hops up and goes to the refrigerator.)* Oh, shit… shitshitshitshitshit… ooooh, c'mon…YES! Thank god. I thought for a sec I might be in a Got Milk? ad. Glass… is this good? When did we buy this? When it says "sell before," that just means that it has to leave the store then, it's not bad by then, right? It smells okay. Fuck it.

He pours a glass and returns to the table, without putting the milk away. LILY rises, goes over to the counter, gets the milk, closes it, puts it back in the fridge, and closes the fridge. She turns and returns to her chair, leaning back, slouched down. She looks at the down left corner of the table.

DONALD

Thanks.

LILY

(Without moving) You're welcome.

LILY gets up and leaves through the stage right door. DONALD looks after her, as if he's about to get up. Opens his mouth as if about to speak. Closes his mouth. Sits still. Lights down.

END

DIG

The stage is covered in sand. About a foot deep if possible. Thick, pale, blue-lit sand so that it shines deep and silver-white. Behind, the drop continues the illusion of an endless expanse of sand, all the way to a late-evening glowing-blue horizon. The horizon is the especially bright shade of blue that shines just before the sky turns black. In tiny, white letters, across the top of the drop: SOVEREIGNTY COLUMNIST.

DIG enters stage right. DIG is wearing a pair of dress pants it looks like he's been wearing for quite some time now. They are of indiscriminate color and the knees have holes. Below the slightly ragged and shortened bottoms of the pants are some ugly black shoes, gray socks above them. Above the pants DIG is wearing an old blazer, buttoned over a wifebeater. He has chest hair.[1] DIG wears a hat.

He crosses to center stage. He walks nonchalantly. This is not an occasion. He has swing. He faces the audience. He delivers:

DIG

(Like a hip hop Steven Jesse Bernstein)
I can't tell the river from the sky.
Can you hold on a sec? I'll be right back
Where I was any minute now.
Any minute now the blood will come,
All wet inside the ears. What's unclear
About that? A smattering of landscape:
If you look around that building
You might just catch a tiny piece of sky.
Is that why I can't sleep?
Everything: you, me, the sidewalk and that bus
We're all waiting for goes to seed.
Is this why it's so bright in here?
The fact remains that it's too bright in here.
Is that why I can't sleep?
It's coming and it's going and it's never going to be
Exactly what we're waiting for.
No, really, I want to know,
What's so unclear about all that?
I'm waiting for you to come back

---

[1] If the actor does not have chest hair, this should *under no circumstances* be faked.

Where I was any minute now.
I'm waiting for that bus.
Where were you when I was last here?
Nothing's really coming to a head
The way we had expected it to be.
A smattering of landscape:
Another day dawning in that sliver of the sky.
Appearance emptiness, God bless it all,
Any minute now we could just go up:
An ascension of smoke and mirrors
In to the river, or is it sky?

DIG waits a minute. He surveys the audience. He takes three steps backwards. He leaves stage right, the way he came.

END

IN THE NICK

There.

Over there.

Do you see it?

It's coming over this way now.

A big anvil cloud of heaven and of ash and

God only knows. A thundercloud of wonderment, some steel in the air.

Don't know where you've been but I bet you've never been anywhere where the
horizon's real.

Little schools of clouds like fishes in the sky: he said that they were the harbingers
of hurricanes

In the Gulf. The water deep and blue inside the seashells of my ears. I never learned
to swim despite everyone's best

Efforts, not even now. Look at that front. It's breaking on the mountaintops. He
never said it in so many words. Truthfully, I was a little girl, and

How should I remember anything but fingertips, monsters made of cloud? That old
anvil cloud is counting time. Gray and white flashes inside now and then—
here it comes now, ready

Or not. This time—who knows?—it could all come down in a shower of rain and
fire. This burning wheel could be the real thing. Did you see that flash?
Count between the lightning and the sound—

Feel the space between you and the air. Hold your breath and count down with
the storm. Did you hear that? Nearer. Up on the ridge, there's a tree that
lightning struck and cleaved it clean in half. My mother

Swore that once the lightning came inside, running down the stovepipe to the
kitchen where she stood. She says that sparks jumped off the stove and she
could feel the air start humming, loud. We should go inside, storm's about
to break.

Open the windows and listen—nothing but a few taps on tin and then it's only
sound and fire. Maybe it will come. Wait. Looks like it's raining
on Cheyenne. Maybe we'll get some of that. Did you hear that? Listen,
maybe we'll get some of that.

PASCAL'S TRIANGLE

First the nothing looks you in the eye.

One the night that wakes me from my sleep.

One the night that wakes me from my sleep.

One the night that wakes me from my sleep.

    Two the pear tree standing on a hill
    When the grass is black and all the leaves are yellow.

One the night that wakes me from my sleep.

One the night that wakes me from my sleep.

    Three the boys that play beneath the bridge,
      Laying still like fishes in the rocks:
    After sunset, in the river's bones.

    Three the girls that walk along the river,
      Pulling flowers from the muddy holes:
    After sunset, in the river's bones.

One the night that wakes me from my sleep.

One the night that wakes me from my sleep.

    Four the glances thrown behind the girl
      As she walks along the beach alone
      As the wind is lifting out her dress,
    Along the boardwalk in the afternoon.

Six the old man sitting on a bench
     Watching the rising tide rush in
          Listening to the footsteps of the girl
          That walks along the boardwalk, along seaside,
     Watching the falling tide escape
  To the horizon, sitting on his bench.

Four the sounds her shoes make on the boards,
  As she walks the beach in afternoon,
  As the wind is lifting out her dress,
Walking down the boardwalk all alone.

One the night that wakes me from my sleep.

One the night that wakes me from my sleep.

Five the stages of the morning light
  Rising from behind the eastward rocks
     Coming over sagebrush towards the fence,
  Lighting up the grass and granite gold
In the stages of the morning light.

  Ten the shivers of the sleeping eye
     Just before the stages of the light
          In the nightly endgame that is dawn
               Coming over sage and eastern rock
                    Quivers underneath the sleeping lid
                    Flutters lashes as the day begins
               Just before the sleeper comes to wake
          In the nightly endgame that is dawn
     Just before the stages of the light
The shivers come into the sleeping mind.

Ten the dreams that come and go in sleep
    As the dreamer turns and returns in his bed
        The dreams of what was then and what has come,
            The dreams that come and go and come again
                As the dreamer moves his restless legs
                    Walking in his mind and pawing at his bed
                Tangled in the sheets and running through his head
            The dreams of what has come from what was then
        As he returns to his turning in his bed
    This dreaming fills the senses through the sleep.

Five the fading of the morning stars
    Dimming in the first-day blue
        Setting, yet a million tiny suns
    Beyond the reach of this, our spinning ground
In the stages of the morning light.

One the night that wakes me from my sleep.

FRACTALS

Night lies low this time of autumn,
Creeps across the streets.

The wriggle and twist of creeping night-life:

> They are invisible,
> They are blind.

The leaves outside shatter yellow, shatter down falling,
Circles of soundless syntax, above the streets.

Sanctified. Inside the silence of release.

At your table, or settling into your bed,
With paper or paints, or your hand on your head,
Symptomatically sinking,
Systematically searching:

The breath becoming rough,
Break, falter and fall. Still,
Unyield, fight, against the drowning, rasp out
Coughs that sound like tin cans full of gravel.

Sinking under the rattle of seconds seeding by:

> You in your chair, sitting,
> As night consumes sitting.

Night swells inside alveoli:
Darkness with the murky consistency of rock oil,
Pooling, clouded gloam in you, and

Looking out—

> The fractal helix of leaves falls
> from above
> In the billion-colored beauty of
> happenstance—

Amianthine algidity,
Or the moonless release of a charnel house.
Unblessed, disintegrating, threadbare,
In the unmitigated infinity of this approaching.

PARLOR GAME

Go ahead,

I say.

It's not like I know how to advise the weather.
My tongue feels like a thistle in my throat.

Thank you.
Sorry.
Nice kicks.

I'm trying to act natural but I think I missed the point.
I feel the dark burn in my stomach where something carved a hole.
Why would anyone want my advice about arrhythmia?
I'm trying to say the right things.
Trouble is, the right things aren't so obvious when you're looking at a
lineup.

I think I'm being stalked by the ontological problem.
I think of the periodic table.
I think of the noble gasses and then I think, "Keep it up, asshole."
Justice is relative, anyway.
Imagine every organism as a symphony, played out in electric surges and syncopated time.
Imagine the holographic safety of the plastic driver's license, now cutting into my hand.
Are you watching closely?
The whole world, laid out before you like pieces of a watch.

LIGHT WARNING

No.

Wait

For it.

You know how

The air feels after everything

Has been carried out, doors and windows closed?

Deep wintertime—I felt the cold coming through the glass, old blade loose

In my left hand. Late at night I used to sit against the window at the far end of my bed

And hope like hell that something would break through. The intimacy of drywall, cold air leaking in. I watched the glass sink through itself inside the windowframe. Sore ribs. I kept on staring through,

As if only waiting. Wheels in the ditch. Body on the wall. Red sky all night that time of year. Where I live now, it never gets that cold. Sometimes, though, when the fires get close enough to let a little ash into the air, I think of windowpanes, and sparks fly out my mouth.

FACTS REMAIN THE SAME

Now?

Now.

I might
Be beginning

To see what you mean.
Ugly ain't the half, that's for sure.
I'd say, more like being unexpectedly sublimed.

Brushfire on the hills behind the sign. Limbo thickening.
I'm still living out of boxes
or just ignoring them. Operating on a crash-by-crash basis,
fumbling, scattershot: chest cavity like a rope bridge giving
way.

ELEVENS TO INFINITY (UPENDED)

I think when you ask for advice, you really want accomplices.

Which applies here, I believe. The kind of woman who advises you, paint your nails black in self-defense, as she rides her

Bike to Hebrew school. I didn't used to need so much hand holding. It's just that now there are all these people whose hands I want to hold. What I'm trying to say

Is, thanks for driving my getaway car. The real advantage to not knowing where you're going is that any road will get you there. That, my friend, is the real prize inside the Cracker Jacks. We're comparing gifts and hooks here, but I think

The parallels are clear. I met a magician last Saturday up in Frisco who summed it all up. Abracadabra, kiddo. So, anyway, after I got off the phone with you, I almost hit a person in a wheelchair. Do you think it's odd they don't put headlights on those things? Never neglect the little things

In life, am I right? You can't just bounce the cripples off your grille. As for what happened later, the nutshell version is, it went about like this: He said, "Thank you." I said, "I'm sorry?" Do you ever feel like you could turn into a dangerous person? After all this, all the advice I have for you is: hunker down. *Semper vigilans* outreaches *semper fi.*

So, last night I saw a picture of your princess in white fur. She photographs well, especially when sucking on her fingers. (Little drunkard.) I understand the devastation of things that will never wind up challenging. I could tell you that the way she spreads her legs is insulting on a whole other level, but we both know it wouldn't get me anywhere. (As if I was trying to get there anyhow.) All apologies, but I digress.

This might be necessary. A litany of cavernous lave-bouche. Actually, a lave-bouche might be better suited to my needs; what you need is a bucket and a rag. I'm sorry, after all. I'm no angel, no martyr, no constipated priest. (No Hamlet, nor was meant to be…) I'm just closing out the work day with some free time on my hands and an unlimited supply of paper. I doubt it matters. Whatever I nail to the door, you don't live here anymore. There's another Santa Ana coming through.

TIME AND SUCCESSION

The first derivative is velocity. The second is acceleration.
The third derivative describes variations in the one before—
Surges and vibrations, hesitations, making all our smallest motions quick.

The distance from here to your shoulder blades takes place in terms of functions.
I'm counting out my pulse as I take measures in my mind,
Counting out the anapests in your collarbone's sway in the wind.

I take derivatives of your position and multiply your body.

I multiply your body by the way your body moves:

The third derivative: an impulse, surge, jolt, super-acceleration—
Changes in momentum of a limited-duration force.
I watch your head tilt a little as the wind picks up.

One hipbone shifts. Shifts the vector of the almost imperceptible—

Keep focused. Count inches over beats,

Now you're feeling for my pulse. There are vectors
In the ache that is shaking in your hands.
You are trying to light my cigarette. You are trying to stay warm.

I know something is breaking now but can't quite calculate what,
Feel the acceleration but have lost the formula for its name.
Arrhythmia, quickening—the metronome I was using for a guide—

Eyes that light darkly: obsidian, beneath clear water, in a creek.
Your palm reaches the hollow edges of my jaw.
Nothing remaining: the coordinates overtake the plane.

RED TEETH

I will be held accountable, but not today.

The weather has been keening for a while, like it might be a national holiday.

Other people's stone-broke scraps of tragedies, frequencies of grief.
I wish I'd studied lamentation more when I'd had the time.

From the roof I can see
another game of cops-and-robbers playing out across the street.
I'm trying to count shots fired. It's a shell game and I lose track.

It's hard to believe how many bullets can be shot at point-blank range before
someone manages to get hit—parsing miracles and chance, I can still hear the
echoes of a playmate's mother telling me about fun and games. Cash and satisfaction;
butchered attempts to find a binary life. The laughs I manage anymore sound more
like failed attempts to cough. Is there a differential diagnosis for a bad choice? I
should have waited for it to come out on video.

The things I will have done tomorrow, the concrete scree that scatters down the hill.
I thought they were apples for a moment, but they're not. These are citrus trees. Gifts,
hooks, a few loose bricks in a pool of broken glass: the man in the far corner only
knows one thing. There's screaming down below but still nobody down—everyone's
trying to explain what's going on. I can't hear anything. They've got gurneys down
there now, all jammed together and angling apart, like a nest of sodden logs, choking
out the narrows of a bending riverbed. I'd like to ask him a question.

$$\Omega = \Omega_m + \Omega_\wedge$$

DO THE MATH

$$\Omega_m$$

One, two, three: creative summation. This isn't something I thought of: ready or not. Outside it's green and gold in chlorophyll and photon-washed colors. Outside, it's sunny like it's about to rain. Green tree, black sky, rain coming. This life right now, this living today. Somewhere, a beautiful girl hangs up the phone. Somewhere, nothing resumes. Somewhere, a star burns out in core collapse and bounces into supernova. This might be happening.

$\Omega_\wedge$

When I was younger and lived where rain was rare, this light was the light of every evening. This golden menacing. When I was playing before dinner in a dirty sandbox besieged by sage, the sky would assume just this posture. In the heartland, sneaking cigarettes on a rooftop; waiting for summer to end. This was how the wind felt. The feeling not of what happens but of what is about to happen. The weather says: Maybe.

$$\Omega_m$$

Fourteen and sunburned with dirty feet on the loading dock, scratching a mosquito bite at the end of the day. Feet brush the tops of the long, dry grass. Where the grass gets deep and deeper green next to the irrigation ditch, the dogs are playing, a tumbleweed of sudden noise. The thunderhead coming from the west is an anvil, they say, sitting in the steel-blue sky. Sitting on the loading dock, the wind on bare shoulders turns cold. Thighs scratch the wood as bare feet scramble inside.

$\Omega_\wedge$

Last night the moon was supposed to have been red. I saw nothing. The red moon
was eclipsed by the earth around ten, only to re-emerge circa one in the morning.
Of course it came back. I sleep with the moon, that is to say, the new moon finds
me soundly sleeping and the full moon keeps me up all night. Diagnose this: tidal
insomnia—now what are you going to do? Don't wait up for me, that's certain.
Certainty being so rare these days, a heavy element and one not often made by stars.
The stars turn hydrogen into helium. The stars turn helium into carbon, carbon
into nitrogen, nitrogen into oxygen, oxygen into silicon, and silicon into iron. The
stars make the elements we are made of. Sometimes, if things get really hot, the
stars turn iron into gold, and then, just to make the alchemists weep, gold into lead.
Somewhere in the Crab Nebula, pencil lead diffuses in great smudgy clouds. Maybe
right now.

$\Omega_{\wedge}$

Right now, the germs might be taking over the world. Your diseases may be the horsemen of a new era, bearing in eons of microbiological dominion. Right now, bacteriophages might be our only hope. Wrap yourself in porcelain, you'll be safe and sound. Bury yourself in diatomaceous earth and wait out the coming storm. On the other end of the phone, the dial tone kicks in. That's the end of something. A white dwarf collecting the folds of its dancing partner's dress, getting ready to explode, which might not be the end of anything.

Ω_m

Sir Almroth Wright is almost right in thinking he's discovered a cure. Typhoid Fever will never be the same. The Boer War provides the perfect opportunity for human testing, and not too many boys die. Sir Almroth Wright has something, him and his autogenous vaccines. Deliver the body of a dead soldier and you can find a way to win the war, or so the metaphor would have you think. The contagion killed in heat, the man killed in fever, and all these bodies left for phagocytosis to destroy.

$\Omega_\wedge$

When you count time, how fast do you count? One, two, three: how long are the breaths you breathe and how long is your voice speaking? I try to keep the numbers spaced out evenly but even so, my breathlessness overtakes me, and by inhalation I stretch time. This expansion like a massive object, this breath like gravity. As the clock leaves the world of its creation, it ticks faster, its tiny tachycardia a release. Somewhere, an event horizon counts down.

$\Omega_\wedge$

Three: in the name of the father, the son, number two and number one, this trilogy
is fading. Somewhere, dinner awaits, cooling in the evening air. What happens thrice?
I'm looking for two numbers, but three isn't one of them. Somewhere, the universe
turns opaque. There's more than three sides to anything. Hell, even our three-
dimensional world is concealing eight more, eleven dimensions like tiny loops of
carpet thread, or ingrown hairs. The Holy Ghost might not be telling you everything.

Ω ^

In the corner of the room, the heater starts up, howling. The joints vibrate and scream. After a minute, the sound diminishes to a whisper, as though passing out or just getting used to it. Outside, the trees are greener now that the sun is gone behind the clouds, and the water has reached the same shade as the sky, two bars of metal cutting the green.

$$\Omega_\wedge$$

Three, two, one: the friction kicks in. Inertia keeps things in, all but friction. But in general, there's no need to stop, we can go on forever and even increase. $\Omega = 1$: we could go on forever. But nothing's slowing down. Everything just keeps on in acceleration, and even the love of our collective life, this little bit of earth and light in transit round a star, remains as distances increase, the things we haven't thought of run away.

DEFINITIONS

FRACTAL

NOUN. A geometric pattern that is repeated at ever smaller scales to produce irregular shapes and surfaces that cannot be represented by classical geometry. Fractals are used especially in computer modeling of irregular patterns and structures in nature.

ETYMOLOGY: French, from Latin *fractus*, past participle of *frangere*, to break.

PASCAL'S TRIANGLE

NOUN. A triangle of numbers in which a row represents the coefficients of the binomial series. The triangle is bordered by ones on the right and left sides, and each interior entry is the sum of the two entries above.

$$
\begin{array}{ccccccc}
 & & & 1 & & & \\
 & & 1 & 2 & 1 & & \\
 & 1 & 3 & 3 & 1 & & \\
1 & 4 & 6 & 4 & 1 &
\end{array}
$$

ETYMOLOGY: After Blaise Pascal.

PRIME NUMBER

NOUN. An integer larger than 1 that has no integral factors but itself and 1.

ETYMOLOGY: *Prime*, originally *pryme*, borrowed from the Old French prime, borrowed directly from Latin *primus*, first, from pre-italic *pris-mos* Indo-European *pris-is-mo-s*.

FIBONACCI VIGNETTE

Here, it is the number of words in a sentence that are counted, with the sentences often being divided between two characters. The number of words in each sentence are the numbers of the Fibonacci sequence, 1, 1, 2, 3, 5, etc.

EUCLID'S ALGORITHM

The unit of measure is the number of words in each character's line. The first two lines establish the numbers on which the algorithm will be run. Then, after the pause, the algorithm is run on the two established numbers, to find the greatest common denominator between them.

EUCLID'S ALGORHYTHM

The same algorithm is being used, only the unit of measure has changed: instead of counting the number of words in a line, count the number of beats.

UNSOLVABLES

Rhinestone Hair Clip, Wendover, They Came Home, and Report From This World all describe problems that are either traditionally unsolvable or unsolved. Wendover is the only one that hasn't yet been solved.

IN THE NICK

The unit of measure is space—nicks—between words. The space before the line, the space at the end of the line, and the space between words are counted. The number of spaces in each stanza is prime, and this poem carries out the sequence of prime numbers: 2, 3, 5, 7, 11, 13, etc.

PASCAL'S TRIANGLE

The numbers of the lines and stanzas carry out the sequence of numbers in Pascal's Triangle, with each stanza representing a single row.

PARLOR GAME, LIGHT WARNING, FACTS REMAIN THE SAME, RED TEETH

All of these are governed by the Fibonacci sequence: something is being counted, and spiraling out accordingly. The units of measure, however, are not always the same.

SPIRAL

The key to reading it straight through is finding the curve of Fibonacci and the Golden Ratio.

FRACTALS

Fractals, etymologically related to the idea of breaking, are associated with chaos and chaos theory.

$$\Omega = \Omega_m + \Omega_\wedge$$

This formula, from astrophysics, relates omega, the fate of the universe to either expand forever or eventually contract, to the relative concentrations of matter and energy in the universe, omega sub m and omega sub lambda, respectively. Current theory places omega roughly equal to one, being made up of about thirty percent matter and seventy percent energy. Thus, the number of segments devoted to matter and the number of segments devoted to energy represent the relative concentrations of matter in the universe in this ten-section prose poem.

---

p. 21 - "Fibonacci Sequence." Hyperdictionary. Webnox Corporation. 20 February 2004. <http://www.hyperdictionary.com/> .

"Algorithm." Oxford English Dictionary Online. Oxford English Dictionary. Feb 20, 2004. < http://80-dictionary.oed.com.ezp2.harvard.edu/>.

"Euclid's Algorithm." Hyperdictionary. Webnox Corporation. 20 February 2004. <http://www.hyperdictionary.com/>.

p. 53 - "Sovereignty Columnist" from *Oxygen* by Aesop Rock

p. 64 - "No Hamlet, nor was meant to be..." ? is from T. S. Eliot's "The Love Song of J. Alfred Prufrock"

p. 78 - "Fractal." American Heritage Dictionary of the English Language, 4th Ed Online. 2001. Houghton Mifflin Co. 20 February 2004. <http://education.yahoo.com/reference/dictionary/>.

p. 78 - "Pascal's Triangle." American Heritage Dictionary of the English Language, 4th Ed Online. 2001. Houghton Mifflin Co. 20 February 2004. <http://education.yahoo.com/reference/dictionary/>.

p. 78 - "Prime Number." Hyperdictionary. Webnox Corporation. 20 February 2004. <http://www.hyperdictionary.com/>.

p. 78 - "Prime." Chambers Dictionary of Etymology. New York: Larousse Kingfisher Chambers Inc, 1988.